Ask Me About It
Daughter of Immigrants

by
Alexandra Juzwiak

To order additional copies of this book, contact:
Xlibris
844-714-8691
www.Xlibris.com
Orders@Xlibris.com

ISBN: Softcover   978-1-6698-2820-4
         EBook   978-1-6698-2819-8

Print information available on the last page

Rev. date: 08/15/2022

Ask Me About It

Daughter of Immigrants

In a classroom, you can feel every emotion. You may feel happy, sad, excited, frustrated, nervous or angry.

During the winter, you can feel a cold rush of air as the school doors open for dismissal. Outside on the blacktop, you can feel the summer heat as the asphalt absorbs the sun and takes it all in. Sometimes, you can even feel a subtle breeze coming from an open window. But you cannot feel what another student is feeling. You can only ask them, "How are you feeling?"

My name is Ola. I *feel* proud to be a first generation United States citizen.

My parents were born in Poland. My sister and I were born in America. Airports are our home. Airplanes allow us to visit our extended family. Long flights, delays and layovers give us endless hours of play, before we get to see our people.

My sister and I liked to imagine that each cloud is a country. Seats at airport gates and on airplanes may seem uncomfortable to most. We learned how to fall asleep in them, using our backpacks and jackets as pillows. I wish someone from school had asked me about all of the planes that my backpack had traveled on.

Because my parents wanted to assure that we could travel back and forth to Poland, we lived in a tiny, yellow, one story home in New Jersey. We could barely fit our family of four, but this meant that we could take turns traveling to see family whenever ticket prices were low. Back in New Jersey, weekends were our designated time to speak with family on the phone.

Friends and family were quick to laugh at or correct my speech. There were times in my life that I felt shy, insecure and frustrated to speak two languages instead of proud. I chose to speak less rather than risk making a grammatical error. Sometimes, it felt like I did not belong to either country. I wish I knew then the uniqueness of my accent.

My name is Ola. I *feel* proud to be a first generation United States citizen.

I can sing two alphabets, both of which consist of tricky digraphs, blending sounds, accent marks and pronunciations.

My sister was the first to experience troubles with homework. Even when my parents wanted to help, a language barrier sometimes made it difficult for them to understand assignments. I wish more people understood what it feels like to be an immigrant or a first generation citizen.

My name is Ola. I *feel* proud to be a first generation United States citizen.

The airport is like an amusement park. First, you have to pack everything that you will need for your adventure, such as your favorite socks, scrunchies and hats. When you arrive at the airport, you head straight towards the check-in kiosk. The staff or computer prints out your ticket for you, which you can later add to your scrapbook of memories.

Security is the first attraction. You wait in line until you reach the x-ray machines, scanners and metal detectors. Then, when it's your turn, you take out any large electronics. You take off your shoes and jacket as fast as you can. You place your personal item and carry-on in the boxes so that they can be scanned. Once you reach the other side of the metal detector, you score yourself to see if that was the fastest time you have ever gone through security.

Next, you search for your gate number. Whoever finds it first is the winner. You are especially lucky if the airport has a flat escalator that allows you to walk even more quickly. There have been many times where we have had to run to our gate, because it was about to close its doors. You cannot be late.

The gate is like a magical tunnel to the tallest roller coaster ride you will ever go on. Once the doors open and airplane staff greets you, you are on your way. Flight attendants, along with pilots, manage the ride and make sure that you are all buckled up and safe through shaky or bumpy turbulence.

My sister and I hate airplane food with a passion. But once we land, everyone claps and cheers for the amazing pilot, stewards and stewardesses. Slowly, we make our way towards international arrivals, where the country's border police will stamp our passports and welcome us.

The baggage claim spins just like a merry-go-round. We compete to see who can spot everyone's belongings. Once we find one of our suitcases, we use all of our strength to try to pick it up, off of the belt. Then, the exit signs are maps that lead us and our baggage to our second home.

My name is Ola. I *feel* proud to be a first generation United States citizen.

20

I attended Polish school from preschool up until high school. Friday nights were designated for evening school, where I could spend time with other immigrant children and embrace our culture. Students there ate the same foods that I did, and shared similar experiences. The nearest school to our house was an hour away, but that did not stop us. My mother still teaches fourth grade and commutes to this day. I wish that all of my teachers knew about my pride in Poland and its history.

There are lots of things you cannot see in a classroom or at school. You cannot see my family, because most of them live in Poland. You cannot see the other immigrant families that celebrate each holiday with us. You may be able to see me, but you cannot see the Polish in me. You may be able to see my lunchbox, but my mother has never packed pierogies, kielbasa or other Polish delicacies for American school. All you can do is ask me about it.

My name is Ola. I *feel* proud to be a first generation United States citizen.

Printed in the United States
by Baker & Taylor Publisher Services